CULLODEN
1746
FIGHT FOR THE THRONE

Chris Tabraham

THE BATTLE
OF CULLODEN
WAS FOUGHT ON THIS MOOR
16TH APRIL 1746.

THE GRAVES OF THE
GALLANT HIGHLANDERS
WHO FOUGHT FOR
SCOTLAND & PRINCE CHARLIE,
ARE MARKED BY THE NAMES
OF THEIR CLANS.

LOMOND
www.lomondbooks.com

Prince Charles Edward Stuart, as a youthful 12-year-old. He was aged 25 when he fought Culloden.

CULLODEN
1746
FIGHT FOR THE THRONE

BACKGROUND TO THE '45

We'll o'er the water and o'er the sea,
We'll o'er the water to Charlie;
Come weal, come woe, we'll gather and go,
And live or die wi Charlie.

Ruthven Barracks, near Kingussie, built in the aftermath of the '15 Jacobite Rising, figured prominently in the '45. Early on, its garrison of redcoats held out against the Jacobites, but surrendered to Gordon of Glenbuchat's men shortly before Culloden. The rump of Prince Charles's army gathered at the barracks after the battle and formally disbanded there two days later.

OVERTHROW OF A DYNASTY

There was much rejoicing in St James's Palace, London, that summer's day in 1688. Mary of Modena had presented her husband, James VII of Scotland and II of England and Ireland, with a baby boy. No matter that rumours were soon circulating that James Francis Edward Stuart was a changeling, smuggled into the royal bed in a warming pan! King James, having endured the heartache of seeing five previous male heirs die in infancy, was overjoyed that here was another who, if the Fates looked kindly upon him, would one day ascend the thrones of Scotland, England and Ireland as James VIII and III.

The Fates decided otherwise. The prospect of a Catholic male heir succeeding to the throne of England united the king's many enemies there. A plot was hatched to overthrow him, and within six months of the happy event, in a bloodless coup King James and Queen Mary were forced to flee to France, taking their son with them. By Christmas Day Prince William of Orange and his wife Mary, James VII & II's eldest daughter by his first queen, had moved into St James's Palace. Though the Stuart dynasty continued to rule, the exiled King James refused to accept his own overthrow. Jacobitism (from the Latin *Jacobus*, for James) was born.

The fight for the throne began almost immediately. Within a month of William and Mary being formally proclaimed joint sovereigns of England and Ireland (13 February 1689), James landed in Ireland and laid siege to Derry. A month later, Scots too had risen up in his name, despite their parliament acclaiming William and Mary from Edinburgh's mercat cross (11 April). Whilst James twiddled his thumbs outside the walls of Derry, Viscount Dundee was raising a Jacobite army in the Scottish Highlands. Four months and 800 miles of marching later, he won a brilliant victory over a government army on the Braes of Killiecrankie (27 July).

To no avail. 'Bonnie Dundee' was tragically killed in the very moment of his victory. Without their charismatic general, the first Jacobite Rising on mainland Britain petered out. Even worse, three days after Killiecrankie,

James was compelled to withdraw from Derry after three months of fruitless endeavour. Less than a year later (1 July 1690), he too was defeated in battle, on the banks of the Boyne, by an army led by King William in person. James returned to France a broken man, and lived out the rest of his days at his court-in-exile, the palace of St Germain-en-Laye, near Paris. And there he died, on 16 September 1701, aged 69.

Jacobitism would have died with him had it not been for the little lad smuggled out of London under his mother's skirts. Prince James assumed the title 'James VIII & III' and his father's cause. His luck was in almost immediately. Within six months of his father's death, William too lay dead. (Queen Mary had predeceased her husband eight years earlier.) James's elder half-sister Anne was now Queen of Scotland, England and Ireland. She too snubbed him, calling him: 'he who pretends to my throne' – whence James's other title 'the Old Pretender'.

But Anne was still without an heir, and at the age of 37 was most unlikely to produce one. The question was – who would succeed her? Of the rag-bag of claimants scattered throughout the royal houses of Europe, two were clear front-runners – Princess Sophia, James VI & I's grand-daughter and wife of the Elector of Hanover, and 'the Pretender' himself. Both were Stuarts, but only one was a protestant.

As far as the English were concerned, Sophia of Hanover it was; anything to avert a Catholic succession. As one Jacobite grandee declared: 'England would as soon have a Turk as a Roman Catholic for a king.' For the Scots the matter was not so clear-cut. James's hopes flickered into life. In 1707 they were positively fanned into flames when, amid much acrimony and recrimination, Scotland and England were united as one sovereign nation. Anne was now queen of Great Britain, and waiting to sit on the throne at her death was the House of Hanover. James was determined that day would never dawn.

JACOBITES AND HANOVERIANS

Help was close at hand, in the person of Louis XIV of France. But Louis' generosity was not entirely born of altruism. Recent heavy defeats in battle against the English had inflicted serious hurt. A Jacobite Rising, he believed, could only distract Britain's attention, and divert vital military resources, from the main theatre of war. Not for the first time would a foreign power use the Jacobites as a pawn on the European chess board.

So it came to pass that on 6 March 1708 James sailed from Dunkirk with five men-of-war and 15 transports packed to the gunnels with 5,000 French troops. Cries of *Vive le Roi* from the quayside rang in his ears. But just as the coast of Fife came into view, so also did the fledgling British Royal Navy. James's plea to be put ashore fell on Admiral Forbin's deaf ears, and by the end of the month he was back on French soil. The second Jacobite Rising was over.

There matters rested until the death of Queen Anne in August 1714, and the accession of her distant cousin, Georg, Elector of Hanover. The 343-year-old Stuart dynasty was at an end. It was just as James V, Mary, Queen of Scots' father, had predicted before his death in 1542: 'It cam wi a lass, it'll end wi a lass.'

The battle of Glenshiel, in Inverness-shire, was the only battle of the little-known, and short-lived, '19 Jacobite Rising. Peter Tilleman's painting depicts General Wightman's redcoats making their final assault on the Jacobite positions. The '19 led to the Hanoverian government raising the six Independent Highland Companies of Foot, more familiarly known as Am Freiceadan dubh *'the Black Watch', in 1725.*

James Francis Edward Stuart at the outset of the 1708 Jacobite Rising; in a painting attributed to Francesco Trevisani. The 20-year-old son of James VII & II was known by Jacobites as 'James VIII & III', and by Hanoverians as 'the Old Pretender'.

Whilst Elector Georg prepared for his coronation as George I, James planned his next bid for the throne. This time there was little prospect of French aid, for Louis had recently negotiated a hard-won peace treaty with Great Britain, a condition of which was that James would have to leave France. James knew support had to come primarily from within his would-be kingdom. And that meant Scotland, for although there were many in England and Wales who would have preferred a Stuart on the throne, it was north of the Border, and particularly among the Catholic and Episcopalian Highland clans, that Jacobitism was strongest. And

that is where the third Jacobite Rising began.

On 6 September 1715 James Erskine, 6th Earl of Mar, raised James's royal standard on the Braes of Mar, in Aberdeenshire. Soon he had a 10,000-strong army at his command, most of them drawn from the traditional clan heartlands. In fact, there was a far wider support among the Highland clans for the '15 than there would be for the '45.

With an army over twice the size of his opponent's, Archibald, Duke of Argyll, Mar advanced on Stirling Castle, and at nearby Sheriffmuir, on 13 November, he demonstrated just how incompetent a general he was. The day-long battle ended in a stalemate, but Argyll was the real victor. By the time James came ashore at Peterhead (22 December), the third Jacobite Rising was all but over. On 4 February 1716 James, the Old Pretender, left Scotland dejected and despairing. He never saw his native land again.

It was the Spanish who financed the fourth Jacobite Rising in 1719. King Philip had found himself in deep trouble in 1718 when both Britain and France turned against him. A Jacobite diversion in Britain would serve his purpose nicely. The plan was to mount a two-pronged attack, the main one in the south-west of England and a diversionary one in the Western Highlands of Scotland. But bad weather and inept planning combined to turn the whole affair into a farce. The main force never even got within sight of Cornwall, let alone land on it. The diversionary force managed somehow to batter its way through the storms – and that is how 300 bemused Spaniards found themselves half way up a mountain in Glenshiel on a sunny June day in 1719, staring at British redcoats freshly arrived from Inverness. By the end of the day, their Jacobite comrades had fled the field, leaving them little choice but to surrender. By the time they were repatriated, Spain had patched up its quarrel with Britain and France. The fourth Jacobite Rising was over.

'BONNIE PRINCE CHARLIE'

The news of the failed '19 Rising made James even more morose. The 'Old Pretender' was fast becoming 'Old Melancholy'. But it wasn't all doom and gloom. Three months after Glenshiel, James married Maria Clementina, daughter of Prince James Sobieski of Poland, and the new 'Queen of Great Britain' duly provided her husband with a son and heir at their new home, the Palazzo Muti, in Rome, on 31 December 1720. They christened him Charles Edward Louis John Philip Casimir Sylvester Maria, but we know him better as the 'Young Pretender' or 'Bonnie Prince Charlie'.

'Dear Carluccio' grew into a high-spirited young man. Though he learned to speak English and French as well as Italian, he was not in the least studious. He much preferred to be outdoors, playing golf and tennis or riding his horse. Aged 14, he had his first taste of warfare when he took part in the siege of Gaeta, south of Rome. He loved it, and the experience probably set him on the course that was to consume him – the fight to reclaim the British throne for the Stuart dynasty.

In January 1744 the 23-year-old Charles told his father that he was going away shooting for a few days. Instead, he headed for Paris, from where he wrote to his father: 'I go, sire, in search of three crowns [Scotland, England and Ireland], which I doubt not to have the honour and happiness of laying at your Majesty's feet. If I fail, your next sight of me shall be in a coffin.' Father and son were destined never to see each other again.

Charles's adventure was no boyish fantasy. Louis XV of France was still smarting from defeat at the hands of the British at the battle of Dettingen the previous year. (Incidentally, Dettingen was the last battle in which a British monarch – George II – commanded his troops in person; thereafter, his third son, William Augustus, Duke of Cumberland, became Commander-in-Chief.) Louis resolved to invade Britain, and by the time Charles

arrived in Paris, 10,000 French troops were embarked on a great fleet ready to sail. Not for the first time, though, bad weather intervened, and by March all were back in port. The '44 Rising was over before it had begun.

Charles should have headed back to Rome there and then, but with characteristic stubbornness he soldiered on. In early July of the following year, 1745, he sailed out of St Nazaire with just two ships (one of which was soon wrecked in action), few arms and even fewer men, bound for Scotland. The famous '45 Jacobite Rising was underway.

Charles Edward Louis John Philip Casimir Sylvester Maria Stuart. The elder son of James Francis Edward Stuart was variously known as 'Bonnie Prince Charlie' or 'the Young Pretender'. The young prince wears the Jacobite 'logo' on his blue bonnet – the white cockade, a rosette or knot of white ribbon.

THE '45: BUILD-UP TO THE BATTLE

Twas on a Monday morning,
Right early in the year,
That Charlie cam to our town,
The young Chevalier.

RAISING THE STANDARD

On 23 July 1745 Charles stepped onto a beach now called *Coileag a' Phrionnsa*, 'the cockle-shell strand of the Prince', on the Outer Hebridean island of Eriskay. They were his first steps on British soil. He was met with little enthusiasm. Those greeting him advised him to go home. 'I am come home', he replied.

But what Charles lacked in men and munitions he more than made up for in charm and charisma. By the time he had stepped onto the British mainland, at Arisaig, two days later, clan chiefs such as Cameron of Lochiel, MacDonald of Clanranald and Macdonnell of Glengarry had been persuaded to 'come out'. Within a month (19 August), at Glenfinnan, in Clanranald country at the head of Loch Shiel, Charles raised his father's royal standard. Around 1,200 clansmen watched as the white, blue and red silk banner was hoisted high into the evening air.

Just three days earlier, the opening shots of the '45 had been fired barely 20 miles away. During a skirmish at the High Bridge, carrying the military road linking Fort William to Fort Augustus over the River Spean, three Royal Scots were killed and another 60 taken prisoner. First blood to the Jacobites.

Recruiting continued in earnest, and when the strength had reached 1,500, Charles moved east. Oh what heady days they were, and what excitement there must have been in the ranks, as they threaded their way through the Western Highlands, round past Fort William and on towards Perth and the Scottish Lowlands, their progress made all the easier courtesy of General Wade's brand-new military roads! The redcoat garrison in Fort William could do little but watch as the Jacobite army marched past. On its triumphant progress to Edinburgh, Prince Charles was lavishly entertained in the ancient Stuart palace at Linlithgow, where the palace fountain ran with claret.

Within a month of leaving Glenfinnan, Prince Charles Edward was holding court, and captivating the ladies, in the grand surroundings of Holyroodhouse, ancient palace of the royal Stuarts in Edinburgh. The sound of merriment therein was in stark contrast to the stony silence emanating from the royal castle barely a mile away. Meanwhile, in Holyrood Park, some 2,500 Jacobite troops awaited their next orders.

DATES WITH DESTINY:
25 July 1745
Prince Charles steps
ashore at Loch nan Uamh
(below), his first time
on the British mainland.
The vessel bringing
him from France,
the Du Teillay, lies
at anchor off-shore.

19 August 1745
In Glenfinnan, at the
head of Loch Shiel
(opposite), the prince
raised his father's royal
standard to begin the
famous '45 Jacobite
Rising.

Prince Charles (centre, on horseback) rides in triumph down the Canongate, Edinburgh, on 18 September 1745; depicted by Thomas Duncan a century later. The handsome, be-tartaned 24-year-old prince was soon captivating the capital's ladies in Holyroodhouse, the ancient royal palace of his Stuart ancestors, at the bottom of Edinburgh's Royal Mile.

ADVANCE INTO ENGLAND

If only Charles had heeded the advice of his lieutenants, who urged him to consolidate his hold on Scotland before venturing south into England, things might have turned out differently. But he didn't. He was anxious to move on, and his audacious victory over general Sir 'Johnny' Cope's redcoats at Prestonpans, 10 miles east of Edinburgh, on the morning of 21 September – all over in the time it took to sing all four verses of the new national anthem *Rule Britannia* – spurred him on. With Scotland recovered for the Stuart dynasty, it was now time to reclaim England. And so he led his victorious army south over the border. By 15 November they had taken Carlisle, and by 30 November Manchester. On 4 December they had reached Derby. And there, at Swarkestone Bridge beside the swirling River Trent, they halted. For Charles the Coronation Chair in Westminster Abbey was now tantalisingly close, barely a week's march away.

But grim reality was fast dawning in Charles's council of war. There had been little outpouring of Jacobite sympathy on the long march south, and even less practical support. Even more worrying, no intelligence had been received that France was about to invade England. Worse still, the Duke of Cumberland, Charles's distant cousin, had been recalled from Flanders with his seasoned troops and taken up a defensive position around Northampton. With General Wade's brigade descending from Newcastle-upon-Tyne, the Jacobite leaders, most of them from the Scottish Highlands, felt uncomfortably vulnerable. Carry on to London – death or glory – or beat a tactical withdrawal to home ground whilst there was still time? For once, Charles's charisma and stubbornness failed to win the day. They turned for home.

WITHDRAWAL TO THE HIGHLANDS

Unbeaten and unbowed, the Jacobite army returned to Scotland in good order. They crossed back over the border on 20 December and entered Glasgow on Boxing Day (26 December). Early in the New Year they won a further victory, this time over Lt. Gen. Hawley's redcoats at Falkirk (17 January 1746). This time the battle lasted fully 30 minutes! But with Cumberland's army hard on their heels, further withdrawal was inevitable. On 1 February the long march back to the Highlands began.

The Jacobite army now split into two divisions. One, comprising the Lowland regiments and the French regulars forming the Irish Brigade, commanded jointly by Lord George Murray and Lord John Drummond, took the coastal route via Perth and Aberdeen. The clan regiments, led by Charles himself, opted for the more direct, but far more arduous, route up over the Drumochter Pass. Despite the shortage of supplies and military equipment, they still contrived to gain further successes. For example, on 11 February Gordon of Glenbuchat's regiment captured the barracks at Ruthven-in-Badenoch, beside the military road near Kingussie, a feat they had failed to achieve on the march south the previous year.

On 20 February Charles's division reached Inverness. They immediately laid siege to Fort George, on Castle Hill, and within hours it was theirs. They blew it up. Within a fortnight they had done the same to mighty Fort Augustus, in the Great Glen, named in honour of William Augustus, Duke of Cumberland. The mounds of smouldering rubble at both sites served as humiliating memorials to the erstwhile might of the House of Hanover in the Highlands. Only Fort William held out.

Cumberland meanwhile had taken the coastal route north, to allow his army to be supplied from the sea. By 27 February he had reached Aberdeen, and there he paused, to let the harsh winter run its course. He grasped the opportunity to forge his troops into a fighting machine capable of combating the clansmen's greatest asset – the feared Highland Charge. Only on 8 April did he resume the advance. Four days later his 7,000 redcoats crossed the treacherous River Spey unopposed and headed west towards Inverness. 'Our men are in high spirits', wrote one of Cumberland's staff officers.

The situation in the opposing camp could not have been more contrasting. The Jacobites were not only exhausted from marching through the winter snows, they were effectively

Wanted!' This government poster published in 1745, satirises 'the Young Pretender', comically depicted in Highland dress and dropping a copy of his Manifesto to the ground. A huge reward of £30,000 was placed on the prince's head.

11

William Hogarth's contemporary painting The March of the Guards to Finchley *satirically depicts a company of Footguards attempting to sober up after a night's heavy drinking in north London on their way to help defend the British capital from the advancing Jacobites. Hogarth is said to have presented his oeuvre to King George II, who refused it, deeming it a sleight on his elite infantry.*

leaderless as well. Charles had long fallen out with his leading general, Lord George Murray. Murray had urged his prince not to engage Cumberland in battle, but to carry out a guerrilla war in the mountains, much as Robert Bruce had done so successfully four centuries earlier. But Charles had stopped listening. Ever since being overruled at Derby, he had retreated more and more into an alcohol-fuelled fantasy world in which he saw God on his side and the French riding to his rescue at the vital moment. The breakdown in trust between the two men would prove Charles's undoing.

On receiving news that Cumberland's army was fast advancing on Inverness, Murray rode out to assess the lie of the land east of the Highland capital. He identified what he believed to be a good defensive position beside a ravine close to Dalcross Castle, but he was overruled. Charles's Irish chief-of-staff, Col. John O'Sullivan, opined that 'it was the worst that

could be chosen for the Highlanders', and offered his own alternative – a spot two miles west of Dalcross on Drummossie Moor, close to Culloden House, the residence of Duncan Forbes, Scotland's Lord Advocate. Murray protested that the boggy moor was 'not proper for Highlanders', on the grounds that it was flat and boggy and therefore not helpful to the main weapon in their armoury, the Highland Charge. Charles brushed aside his protestations: 'God damn it! Are my orders still disobeyed?'

And so it was that on the morning of Tuesday 15 April 1746 less than 6,000 half-starved Jacobite troops filed onto bleak, windswept Drummossie Moor. And there they stood, awaiting the enemy's appearance. But the enemy never showed. Even though they had reached Nairn, a morning's march away, by Monday 14 April, Cumberland had ordered another halt. This time it wasn't the bad weather holding him back; he was celebrating his 25th birthday!

By noon Charles knew there would be no battle on the moor that day. So he decided to take the fight to Cumberland. Convinced that he would catch his celebrating cousin off guard, he ordered a daring night attack on the redcoats' camp. And so, in the gathering gloom, the Jacobite army filed off the field and headed for Nairn 12 miles to the east. It was a huge mistake. Several hours later, in the cold light of dawn, the cold reality of their predicament was obvious; they were still over two miles away from their target. Realising that the precious element of surprise had been lost, Murray ordered the 'about turn', and the Jacobites, by now even more exhausted and hungry than before, slowly trudged their way back to Culloden.

No sooner had the men sunk into their rain-sodden sleep in the grounds of Culloden House than news arrived of the enemy's approach. The skirl of the bagpipes aroused them from their brief slumber and, for the second time in 24 hours, the Jacobites prepared to march up onto the moor. It was Wednesday 16 April 1746. The battle of Culloden was about to begin.

'A view of ye Scotch & French champ in Scotland, 1746' offers a rare glimpse of the Jacobite army in camp. The depiction of women and children in the foreground confirms that battles weren't exclusively a male preserve.

DIVIDED LOYALTIES

Culloden is often seen today as yet another war between Scotland and England. It was not. Culloden was the culmination of a bloody civil war in which nationality played only a minor part. At Culloden Scot was set against Scot, Highlander against Lowlander, Highlander against Highlander. In addition to Ballimore's Highlanders, most of them Campbells, three Scottish-raised regiments fought on the government side – Campbell's Fusiliers (who would become the Royal Scots Fusiliers), St Clair's Royals (later the Royal Scots), and Sempill's (later the King's Own Scottish Borderers). Among Sempill's ranks were Highlanders seconded from the Black Watch Regiment, attired in their government-issue tartan.

Members of the same family fought each other that fateful day too. The son and heir of the chief of Clan Farquharson, for example, fought on the government side against his own clan regiment. Then there was young Roderick Chisholm, who commanded his father's clansmen. Had he not been killed early on in the charge he would have found himself coming up against two of his elder brothers, John and James, both serving as captains in the Royals. After the battle his siblings would have searched up and down the blood-stained battlefield for their wee brother's body.

THE COMBATANTS AND BATTLE ORDER

THE JACOBITE ARMY

Commander-in-Chief
Prince Charles Edward Stuart – aged 25

Escort Troop: Lord Elcho's Lifeguards and Fitzjames's Horse (32 men)

Chief of Staff: Col. John William O'Sullivan

Commanding Officers: Lord George Murray; Lord John Drummond; James Drummond, Duke of Perth; Col. John Roy Stewart; Col. Sir John MacDonald

FOOT – Front Line: Athollmen (500); Lochiel's Regiment (650); Appin Regiment (150); Lovat's Regiment (500); Lady Mackintosh's Regiment (500); Monaltrie's Battalion (150); MacLeans and MacLachlans (182); Chisholm's Regiment (100); Clanranald's Regiment (200); Keppoch's Regiment (200); Glengarry's Regiment (500)

Second Line: Lord Lewis Gordon's Regiment (500); Lord Ogilvy's Regiment (500); John Roy Stewart's Regiment (200); Kilmarnock's Footguards (200); Glenbuchat's Regiment (200); Duke of Perth's Regiment (200); Irish Picquets (302); Royal Ecossois (350)

HORSE – Fitzjames's Horse (70); Lord Elcho's Lifeguards (30); Bagot's Hussars (36); Strathallan's Horse (30)

ARTILLERY – 11 x 3-pounders + 1 x 4-pounder (c.10)

Total no. of fighting men = max. 6300

THE GOVERNMENT ARMY

Commander-in-Chief
Prince William Augustus, Duke of Cumberland – aged 25

Escort Troop: Duke of Cumberland's Hussars (c.20 men)

Chief of Staff: Lt. Gen. Henry Hawley

Commanding Officers:
Major Gen. Humphrey Bland;
Major Gen. William Anne, Earl of Albemarle;
Major Gen. John Huske;
Major William Belford

FOOT – Front Line: Barrell's (4th Foot) (325); Monro's (37th Foot) (426); Campbell's (21st Fusiliers) (358); Price's (14th Foot) (304); Cholmondley's (34th Foot) (339); St Clair's (1st Royal Foot) (401)

Second Line: Wolfe's (8th Foot) (324); Ligonier's (59th/48th Foot) (325); Sempill's (25th Foot) (429); Bligh's (20th Foot) (412); Fleming's (36th Foot) (350); Howard's (3rd Foot) (413)

Reserve: Pulteney's (13th Foot) (410); Battereau's (62nd Foot) (354); Blakeney's (27th Foot) (300); Ballimore's Highlanders (200)

HORSE – Cobham's (10th Dragoons) (276); Ker's (11th Dragoons) (300); Kingston's (10th Horse) (211)

ARTILLERY – 10 x 3-pounders + 6 x Coehorn mortars (106)

Total no. of fighting men = max. 6600

A depiction of the battle by the government's official war-artist, David Morier, entitled An Incident in the Rebellion of 1745. *Some incident! The men of Clan Chattan (Lady Mackintosh's Regiment), sporting their blue bonnets with white cockades, engage with the redcoats of Barrell's Regiment (4th Foot).*

THE JACOBITE ARMY:
WHAT THEY LOOKED LIKE

CLANSMAN: He wore little but his shirt, plaid, bonnet, sporran and brogues. The plaid (Gaelic *feileadh mór* 'big wrap') was a woollen cloth several yards long, fixed over one shoulder to leave the sword arm free. The rest was wrapped around the body down almost to the knees. On the march it served as a blanket. His blue bonnet bore his clan badge and the white cockade. In his sporran he carried any valuables and his daily ration of oatmeal. He was armed with a broadsword, targe (shield) and dirk (dagger). The targe was about 50 cm in diameter, made of two layers of wood, the grain of one laid across the other, and the whole covered in cow hide. It had a central metal boss and brass studs. The long-bladed dirk was carried in a leather sheath attached to the belt. By the time of Culloden, he might also have acquired a musket, and perhaps a pair of pistols.

THE GOVERNMENT ARMY:
WHAT THEY LOOKED LIKE

REDCOAT: He got his nickname from the red coatee he wore over a red waistcoat. His breeches were mostly red also. Only his gaiters were white. Each regiment was distinguished by different colours, displayed on the coat's cuffs and facings, and on the cap. The elite grenadiers wore conical caps with GR (for Georgius Rex) embroidered on them, whilst the regular companies wore the tricorn (three-cornered hat). Each man was armed with a flintlock musket known as a 'Brown Bess'. Its 46"-long steel barrel fired a 1¼-ounce lead ball, and was fitted with a socket bayonet with a triangular 17" blade. The bayonet normally hung from a buff leather belt, along with a sword. Ammunition was carried in a black cartridge box worn over the left shoulder. Each man also carried a knapsack, linen bread bag and tin canteen.

THE BATTLE OF CULLODEN

(WEDNESDAY 16 APRIL 1746)

Drummossie Moor! Drummossie day!
A waefu day it was to me;
For there I lost my father dear,
My father dear, and brethren three.

OPENING SHOTS

The exhausted Jacobite army slowly filed from Culloden up onto the wet moor and formed into line, but not before an unseemly argument had taken place over who should have the honour of holding the right wing. Ever since Bannockburn in 1314, Clan Donald had taken that coveted position, and indeed had done so at both Prestonpans and Falkirk. But not this day. Lord George Murray had claimed that right, and for once Charles let him have his way.

Thus it was that Murray led his brigade onto the moor first – the Athollmen (a mix of Stewarts, Murrays, Robertsons, Menzies and Macgregors), Lochiel's Regiment (Camerons) and the Appin Regiment (mostly Stewarts and Maclarens). Next followed Lord John Drummond's brigade – Lovat's Regiment (Frasers), Lady Mackintosh's Regiment (Clan Chattan, comprising mainly Mackintoshes, Macgillivrays and Macbeans), Monaltrie's Regiment (Farquharsons), a regiment of assorted MacLeans and Maclachlans, and Chisholm's Regiment. It fell to the affable Duke of Perth to lead the three MacDonald regiments, Clanranald's, Keppoch's and Glengarry's, still smarting from the slight done to them, onto the left wing.

The second line then took up position 100 metres to their rear. Col. John Roy Stewart's brigade formed the centre – the Duke of Perth's Regiment, Glenbuchat's Regiment, Kilmarnock's Footguards, his own regiment, Lord Ogilvy's Regiment and Lord Lewis Gordon's Regiment. On their flanks were the two regiments of the Irish Brigade, the Irish Picquets behind Clan Donald and the Royal Ecossois behind Murray's brigade. These Scots exiles serving with the French regular army, and seconded to Charles's army for the duration of the '45, must have presented a stark contrast to the clan regiments around them, dressed as they were in their smart red (Irish Picquets) and blue (Royal Ecossois) coatees.

With their paltry battery of guns in front, and their equally meagre cavalry to left and right, there they stood, Prince Charles Edward Stuart's bedraggled, exhausted army, now numbering less than 6,000 men, in the strengthening drizzle and gathering gale. Their clergy led them in prayer. With the words of Psalm 20 ringing in their ears – 'Give victory to the king, O Lord; answer us when we call.' – they made ready to take on all that His Royal Highness William Augustus, Duke of Cumberland, could throw at them.

Precisely what Cumberland had at his disposal soon became clear enough. Around the time the weary Jacobites were returning to Culloden from their abortive night march, Cumberland's sergeants were going among

William Augustus, Duke of Cumberland, at Culloden in an 18th-century portrait by David Morier. Cumberland fought alongside his father, George II, at Dettingen (27 June 1743), and was appointed Captain-General and Commander-in-Chief early in 1745. The portly prince lost three of the four battles he commanded (Fontenoy – 11 May 1745, Lauffeld – 2 July 1747, and Hastenbeck – 21 July 1757). His sole victory was Culloden. He died unmarried in 1765 aged just 44.

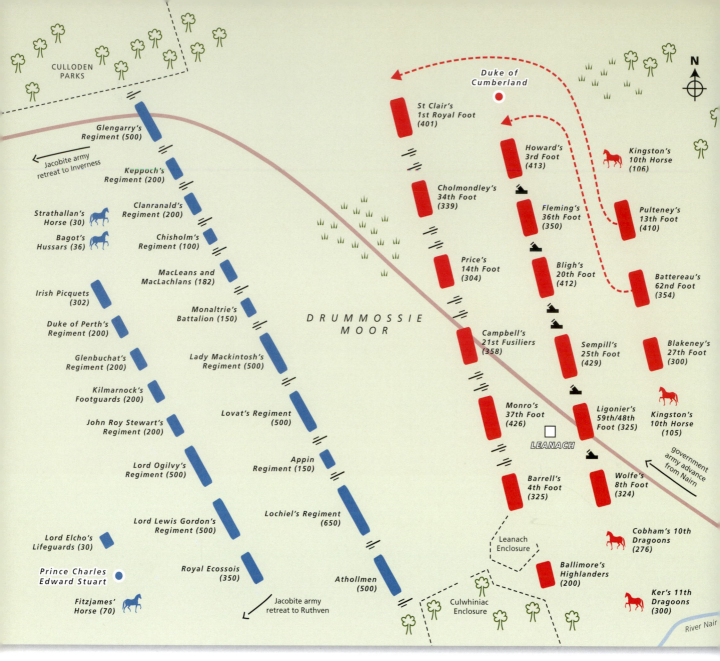

Plan of the battlefield showing the initial dispositions of the armies, the Jacobites (blue) on the left and the government troops (red) on the right. Before the Jacobites charged, Cumberland ordered two of his three reserve regiments – Battereau's and Pulteney's – to take up positions on the forward right.

their men rousing them from their good night's sleep. By beat of drum the redcoats formed into their columns for the three-hour march to the moor. By 11 o'clock that morning, Cumberland's 15 regiments of foot and 800 dragoons began filing onto the field of battle 'like a deep sullen river'.

Cumberland's chosen battle order was for three lines. The first, commanded by the Earl of Albemarle, comprised six regiments (from left to right): Barrell's, Monro's, Scots Fusiliers, Price's, Cholmondley's and the Royals. Forming Major Gen. John Huske's second line were another six: Wolfe's, Ligonier's, Sempill's, Bligh's, Fleming's and Howard's. The three

remaining regiments – Blakeney's, Battereau's and Pulteney's – he held in reserve in the third line, together with Kingston's Horse. The rest of the Horse, and Ballimore's Highlanders, made up mostly of Campbells, assembled some distance to the left of the main body. Cumberland rode along the lines making his final inspection before taking up his position on the right flank, behind the Royals.

No sooner were all assembled when Cumberland was brought intelligence that the enemy were showing signs of changing their deployment. So it was, but this was no comprehensive redeployment. Murray, on the Jacobite right, having noted that the Leanach

enclosure jutting into the field of battle would impede his brigade's charge, had wheeled his men round a little to the north. Cumberland, thinking that his own right flank was becoming increasingly vulnerable to the Highland Charge, ordered Battereau's and Pulteney's to take up positions on the right of the first and second lines, leaving just Blakeney's in reserve.

By noon the two armies were in place, their lines stretching for over 1,000 metres across the moor on a roughly NW – SE axis. After six months of pursuit the length of Britain, barely 600 metres of rough ground now separated Cumberland from Charles. Infrequent visits of the pale spring sunshine occasionally glinted off a bayoneted musket here, a brandished broadsword there. But the weather was worsening by the minute, the drizzle turning to rain and the wind strengthening from the east. When the time came to charge, the clansmen would have icy sleet driving into their faces as well as round shot and musket balls. As the situation grew graver by the minute, Murray turned to Cameron of Lochiel and muttered the prophetic words: 'We are putting an end to a bad business.'

It was the Jacobites who fired the opening shots. Cumberland, a portly fellow, was not going to let a battle interfere with his luncheon! But the sound of the Jacobites' 3-pounders firing a ragged opening salvo brought a swift response, and soon Major Belford's field-guns were wreaking havoc and destruction in the Jacobite ranks. When one young man standing close to Charles was cut in two by a cannonball, the Prince was persuaded to make his way to the comparative safety of the rear.

For around ten minutes Belford's guns and mortars poured forth their murderous contents. It was too much for the clansmen in the front line. In the absence of the order to attack from their commander-in-chief, they took the matter into their own hands. They lurched forth 'like troops of hungry wolves', wrote an Ayrshire man fighting with St Clair's 1st Royal Foot.

This somewhat stylised print of Culloden was among the first published after the battle. The mounted Duke of Cumberland is depicted (foreground, centre right) directing operations from the rear of the redcoat lines, when in fact he took up position on the right wing, behind St Clair's (1st Royal Foot).

After enduring a murderous opening 10-minute onslaught from Major Belford's heavy guns (see opposite), the clansmen charge towards the government lines before stopping some 50 metres short to fire off their muskets (above).

CHARGE!

Doubt surrounds precisely who gave the order to advance. One eye-witness, though, was in no doubt as to where the famous Highland Charge began. Lt. Col. Joseph Yorke, one of Cumberland's staff officers, told how: 'they broke from the centre in three large bodies, like wedges, and moved forward', thus pointing the finger of suspicion at Clan Chattan (Lady Mackintosh's Regiment), commanded by Alexander Macgillivray of Dunmaglas.

Where Clan Chattan led, the rest followed. But just as Lord George Murray had suspected, the walled Leanach enclosure on their right flank forced his brigade left into the path of Clan Chattan. The resulting melée was just what the feared Highland Charge did not need. Even worse, for some unexplained reason, Clan Donald out on the Jacobite left took some time to enter the fray. Charles's chief of staff, Col. O'Sullivan, who had positioned himself there, told of how their brigade commander, the Duke

'CLAYMORE!' – THE HIGHLAND CHARGE

The main weapon in the Jacobite army's armoury was the feared Highland Charge, a tactic unique to the clansmen. Angus MacDonald's islesmen had used it to powerful effect at Bannockburn in 1314 to help secure victory for King Robert Bruce. In those days the clansmen wielded a spear or axe, but by the time of the Jacobite Risings the broadsword had become their main weapon.

Advancing towards the enemy at a trot, pipers and all, they stopped about 50 metres short and fired their muskets. Casting them aside, they then made a final dash for the opposing line, shouting 'Claymore' (Gaelic for 'great sword': *claidheamh*, sword and *mór*, great) and screaming wildly, their swords held high, their targes protecting their

upper body from incoming musket fire. On engaging with the enemy, they used their targes to deflect the enemy bayonets whilst they wielded their broadswords in offence. In close hand-to-hand fighting they unsheathed their dirks and used them for stabbing.

To help counter the Highland Charge, the Duke of Cumberland, on the long march north, had instructed his officers to teach each redcoat not to thrust his bayonet at the man directly in front of him, but at the exposed flank of the man to his right. This tactic may well have had a bearing on the outcome. In any event, the battle of Culloden was the last occasion the feared Highland Charge was used in pitched battle.

of Perth, was reduced to seizing Clanranald's colours and yelling that he would call himself a MacDonald thereafter if they would but follow him. With a certain reluctance, they too ventured forth. The great surge forward that was the celebrated Highland Charge quickly became a bunched, broken and ragged line.

As the advancing clansmen closed to within 300 metres of the government lines, they came under remorseless fire from Major Belford's heavy guns ranged against them. By now Belford had ordered his artillerymen to change from cannonball to grape shot (canisters full of lead shot), and this was soon making 'open lanes through them, the men dropping down by wholesale.' Cameron of Lochiel was among the first to be felled, both his ankles smashed to smithereens.

As they closed to within 50 metres, those with muskets fired and discarded them before charging screaming at the enemy. Lt. Col. Yorke continued his gory narrative: 'At first they made a feint, as if they would come down upon our right, but seeing that wing so well covered, and imagining that they might surround the left because they saw no cavalry to cover it, two of those wedges bore down immediately

upon Barrell's and Monro's regiments, which formed the left of the first line; and after firing very irregularly at a considerable distance, they rushed furiously in upon them, thinking to carry all before them, as they had done on former occasions.'

Now was the time when all those weeks of drilling back in Aberdeen in March would be put to the test. As the screaming horde rapidly approached, Barrell's and Monro's redcoats levelled their muskets and fired, then reloaded and fired again right at the very moment

Having discharged, then discarded, their muskets, the clansmen resume their headlong charge at the government lines, screaming 'Claymore!'. Within seconds they are upon them, but only after a second volley of musket fire from the redcoats takes its dreadful toll.

The redcoats in the front line, having fired their second volley of musket-fire into the rapidly advancing clansmen, use their bayonets to fend off the first wave, thus allowing their comrades behind to reload their muskets and fire off further volleys. Among the many casualties is Macgillivray of Dunmaglas, commanding officer of Clan Chattan.

of impact. One redcoat told of hundreds of clansmen falling at that first volley.

But their momentum was by now so great that those still standing in Clan Chattan's ranks thundered into the government's left, quickly followed by Murray's Athollmen and Camerons. Barrell's 325 men took the full brunt and were burst apart. Monro's men too buckled under the intense pressure. Through the gap the clansmen stormed 'in a cloud', before crashing into Sempill's regiment in the second line. All was bedlam, shouts of anger and cries of despair ascended into the early afternoon air in equal measure. One account tells of a Macgillivray hacking down a dozen redcoats before falling. An officer from Monro's later recounted that 'our lads fought more like devils than men'. One of Barrell's privates described his experience too: 'It was dreadful to see the enemies' swords circling in the air. And to see the officers of the army, some cutting with their swords,

others pushing with spontoons, the sergeants running their halberds into their opponents' throats, the men ramming their fixed bayonets in up to their sockets.'

In that first, bloody encounter, Cumberland's army suffered by far the bulk of the casualties it would take that day – 31 killed and 176 wounded, out of a total of 50 dead and 259 wounded. Among the fallen was Lord Robert Ker, of Barrell's, his head 'cleft from crown to collar-bone'. Barrell's commanding officer, Lt. Col. Robert Rich, lost a hand as he did his utmost to cling on to the regimental colours.

But these losses were as nothing compared with the casualties sustained by the Jacobites. Of Clan Chattan's 21 officers, all but three were killed. They included Macgillivray of Dunmaglas himself, their commanding officer, who managed somehow to crawl to the aptly-named Well of the Dead before succumbing to his many wounds. It is possible that as many as

700 clansmen fell in those opening moments. What is sure is that the vast majority of the total Jacobite dead of around 1,200 were the result of that initial dreadful engagement.

With the full horror unfolding before their eyes, Clan Donald fast approached the government lines, their progress having been impeded both by the boggier ground they had had to cross and the additional distance they had had to cover. They never had the opportunity to engage with the enemy in hand-to-hand fighting though. Unlike Barrell's and Monro's regiments, who barely had time to fire off two musket rounds, the men of Pulteney's Regiment and the Royals out on the government right flank were able to pour an unrelenting hail of bullets into the advancing clansmen. Cumberland himself, standing close to them, described how 'the Royals and Pulteney's hardly took their firelocks from their shoulders'. Among the killed was MacDonald of Keppoch. Clanranald was among the injured. The remaining MacDonalds, denied the chance to put their broadswords and dirks to deadly use, and having discarded their muskets after one volley, were reduced to throwing stones at the redcoats.

Somehow, amid all the carnage around him, Lord George Murray had contrived to stay alive, despite losing his horse and breaking his sword. Seeing the hopelessness of the situation he fought his way out of the fray in an attempt to bring in the Jacobite second line. He found the cupboard almost bare. Only Kilmarnock's Footguards, the Irish Picquets and Royal Ecossois remained in position, for by now Lord Ogilvy's and Lord Lewis Gordon's regiments were doing their utmost to fend off a flanking manoeuvre by Cobham's and Ker's dragoons on their right flank. 'All is going to pot', declared O'Sullivan. He was spot on. The end was nigh.

The close-ordered ranks of the government first line are soon burst apart by the charging clansmen. In the ensuing bedlam, redcoats are cut to pieces by the whirling broadswords of the clansmen, who in turn are rammed by the redcoats' bayonets and halberds. Over 700 Highlanders are killed in those opening murderous minutes.

Gradually, the superior numbers and firepower of the government army take their toll, helped by the inability of the Jacobite left wing to engage in close-quarter fighting. Despite heavy losses, and with the corpses of their slaughtered comrades piling up around them on the boggy moor, the remaining clansmen fight on.

DEFEAT

Scarcely had Murray brought Kilmarnock's Footguards and the Royal Ecossois into the action than the rout began in earnest. Chevalier de Johnstone, Murray's Edinburgh-born aide-de-campe, stared aghast at the scene fast unfolding before his eyes: 'I saw nothing but the most horrible of all spectacles; the field of battle, from the right to the left of our army covered with Highlanders dispersed and flying as fast as they could to save themselves.'

He was not alone. Charles too looked on in horror. O'Sullivan urged his commander-in-chief to withdraw, but Charles seemed reluctant, shouting at the retreating clansmen to return to the fray. Only when Cumberland's dragoons began to appear did he think fit to leave the field. Lord Elcho yelled at his prince's fast retreating rear: 'There you go for a damned, cowardly Italian!'

As the clansmen fled the field, the massed ranks of the Irish Picquets and Royal Ecossois did their utmost to cover their retreat. The Picquets on the left wing bravely confronted Cobham's Dragoons before withdrawing behind the comparative safety of Culloden House's estate wall, in the process sadly losing their commanding officer, Lt. Col. Walter Stapleton. The Royal Ecossois attempted a similar stalling manoeuvre over on the battered right wing, but as they inched back alongside the boundary wall of the Culwhiniac enclosure, firing volleys into the advancing Scots Fusiliers as they did so, they came under fire from an unexpected source. Hidden from sight behind the dyke, Ballimore's Highlanders were taking pot-shots at them. Unbeknown even to Cumberland, who had given strict instructions that the Campbells, the only Highland clan regiment in the government ranks that day, be kept out of the action, Capt.

Colin Campbell of Ballimore had brought his men up for a taste of the action. Alas, he too fell dead upon the moor.

By this time Cumberland's infantrymen had done their work. It was the turn now of his cavalry to finish off the job. As Cobham's Dragoons and Kingston's Horse began to sweep across the moor from the north, Lt. Gen. Henry Hawley slipped the leash off his own dragoons stationed to the south. Many spurred after the Jacobites fleeing down the Inverness road, mercilessly cutting them down with their swords. 'It was a ghastly sight to see', wrote one dragoon, 'some dead, some tumbling and wallowing in their blood, others not quite dead crying for mercy. We followed and slew them for three miles till the Dragoons were quite gutted with gore.'

Gradually, an eerie stillness descended on the moor, the silence broken only by the groans of the injured and dying. After giving them time to recover from their ordeal, Cumberland rode among the regiments of foot, hailing his brave men. Then he ordered them to advance and take possession of the field. As they reached the Jacobites' starting position, they halted briefly and huzzaed loudly. They then moved on down the road. By 4 o'clock that afternoon Cumberland was in Inverness.

In their wake around 1,500 Jacobites lay dead or dying on the windswept moor – men who had worn the blue bonnet and white cockade with pride. And trampled into the boggy, blood-stained ground that awful April day, alongside the discarded broadswords and targes of the clansmen, was the last, lingering hope that the ancient Stuart dynasty might come to reign again. The battle of Culloden – the last pitched battle fought on British soil – was over. From first to last it had taken less than an hour.

With defeat staring them in the face, and with the added complication of Cumberland's dragoons now entering the fray, the remaining clansmen turn and flee the field. Prince Charles likewise decides it is time to beat a hasty retreat. After less than an hour the last pitched battle to be fought on British soil is over.

END OF THE DREAM

Their winding-sheet's the bluidy clay,
Their graves are growing green to see;
And by them lies the dearest lad
That ever blest a woman's ee!

AFTERMATH

The battle itself was not the last Culloden Moor saw of the action. Barely had the gun smoke cleared from the boggy heath than the so-called 'vestry men', those redcoats deemed unfit to serve in the front line but capable of 'battlefield clearance' duties, went about the blood-drenched moor, mercilessly despatching those Jacobites still writhing and groaning from their wounds. They were joined in their gory work by the female 'camp-followers' in Cumberland's army, relieving the fast-stiffening corpses of their valuables. For the next two days both went about their gory, gruesome work.

Nor did the killing end on Culloden Moor. In truth, by far the greater slaughter had yet to begin. Stories of atrocities by Cumberland's army in the aftermath of the battle are legion and legendary. One tells of 30 clansmen being burned alive after the barn they had taken shelter in was torched; those attempting to save themselves ran from the inferno only to be impaled on the point of a bayonet. Another recounts how 20 Jacobites sheltering in Culloden House were taken out by their countrymen serving in St Clair's Royals, lined up against a wall and shot. Nowhere in the vicinity of the battlefield was safe from the avenging redcoats.

Yet still the killing went on. Cumberland was so determined to ensure that the Jacobites would never again threaten his father's throne that he embarked on reprisals that were as brutal as they were indiscriminate. After drawing breath in Inverness, he was off once more, leading his army down the Great Glen to Fort Augustus like a tornado. Search parties were sent into the hills and glens 'to pursue and hunt out these vermin amongst their lurking holes'. Whole townships were ruthlessly cleared, the rude croft houses of the clansmen 'burnt to ashes, their wives and daughters ravished'. Farming and fishing gear were destroyed, and thousands of livestock stolen; 8,000 head of cattle alone were driven off the hills and into Fort Augustus in those first few weeks. There were even reports of redcoats looting and destroying the churches of the Catholic and Episcopalian clansmen.

To the roll-call of Culloden's 1,500 dead were now added countless more; the exact

An estimated 1,500 Jacobites died either on the battlefield (below), or as they fled towards Inverness. Of the 3,500 taken prisoner, 120 were hanged, 600 died in captivity, and 1,000 were deported. Just over 1,000 were subsequently freed. J. E. Millais' painting of 1853, Order of Release *(opposite), shows a clansman being reunited with his barefoot wife, who hands the release document to the redcoated guard.*

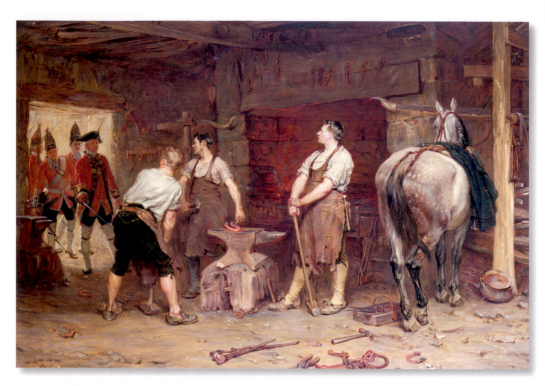

Within hours of the battle, Cumberland's redcoats were combing the Highland straths and glens searching for so-called 'rebels'. They also did their utmost to hunt down 'the prince in the heather'. J. S. Lucas's late 19th-century painting After Culloden: Rebel Hunting *depicts grenadiers about to search a blacksmith's premises. Englishmen such as Lucas instinctively used the pejorative word 'rebel'.*

number will never be known. A further 3,500 were sent to rot in English gaols and prison hulks or were transported to the West Indies and other colonies 'outside our dominions'. The lords Kilmarnock and Balmerino, both captured at Culloden, were taken to London, tried, found guilty and beheaded. Another 120 clansmen were hung from the rope.

For three months Cumberland remained in the Highlands supervising the slaughter. When he returned south to London that July, he was given a hero's welcome. His grateful father created him Baron Culloden, and George Frederick Handel composed the rousing anthem *See the Conqu'ring Hero Comes* in his honour. They even named a pretty flower after him – 'Sweet William'. Jacobites, though, preferred to call him 'Stinkin' Billie' after a weed. Back in the Scottish Highlands the clansmen knew him simply as 'the Butcher'.

Even after Cumberland's departure, the terror continued, this time orchestrated not from Fort Augustus but from distant Westminster. What Parliament decreed was nothing short of a blatant denial of basic human rights. The Jacobite chiefs were stripped of their estates and their powers of jurisdiction.

Their clansmen were simply stripped, forbidden by a petty Disarming Act from carrying weapons and wearing kilts – even playing the bagpipes!

And just in case they thought about rising up again, from a barren shingle spit jutting into the Moray Firth near Ardersier, almost within sight of the battlefield, rose a formidable new garrison fortress armed with over 90 guns and holding 2,000 redcoats. The army named it Fort George, in honour of the 'rightful' king.

The measures, trivial or no, had their desired effect. Culloden and its bloody aftermath finally put paid to the ancient clan system, and any lingering claim to authority and independence their chiefs might have clung to. Mighty Fort George was never called on to fire a single shot in anger.

'THE PRINCE IN THE HEATHER'

Whilst, after the battle, individual clansmen did their best to return to their crofts in the western Highlands, those serving in the Lowland regiments, around 1,000 men, contrived to retire in reasonable order, cross the River Nairn to the south of Drummossie Moor and head by way of Corrybrough to Ruthven

Barracks 40 miles away to the south-west. There they were joined by around 500 clansmen of Euan Macpherson of Cluny, who had been unable to make the battlefield in time.

It was at Ruthven, two days later, that Lord George Murray received a hastily-scrawled note from Charles instructing that each man 'shift for themselves' – in other words, it was every man for himself. It was a harrowing moment for each and everyone of them, given all that they had endured. Chevalier de Johnstone wrote of the Highlanders giving 'vent to their grief in wild howlings and lamentations; the tears flowed down their cheeks...' After some brave words about regrouping and carrying on the fight, common sense prevailed. On 18 April, in the shadow of the Hanoverian barracks, the Jacobite army formally disbanded. After 242 days, the '45 Rising was over.

What of Charles himself? After leaving the field, he too headed south-west, accompanied by the ever-loyal O'Sullivan. They headed deep into Fraser country on the eastern shore of Loch Ness, before passing through Fort Augustus and up over the mountains to the Atlantic coast. Having openly declared on the battlefield that 'they won't take me alive', Charles's only thought now was to get back to France as quickly as possible.

But bad luck continued to dog his every step. On reaching Loch nam Uamh, 'loch of the caves', close to where he had first landed the previous year, he saw no evidence that French ships were in the area. He was persuaded to cross to the Outer Hebrides, in the belief that Stornoway offered a better prospect of escape. Just four days after embarking on his treacherous voyage across the Minch, two French frigates, the *Mars* and the *Bellone*, nosed into Loch nam Uamh. If only Charles had not been in such haste, he would have been back in Paris within a month of Culloden. Instead, he would have to endure another four months and more living as a fugitive. The romantic story of 'the prince in the heather' was about to begin.

Charles and O'Sullivan never made it to Stornoway. Such was the ferocity of the storm-lashed seas that they were tossed ashore on Benbecula. It was now Sunday 27 April. For the next seven weeks Charles remained in hiding in the Outer Hebrides. Yet still 'Lady Luck' refused to come to his aid. Within days of his arrival, he suffered yet another profound disappointment when he spied the *Mars* and *Bellone* heading back out to the open sea. Alas, they failed to see him and sailed on by.

After moving clandestinely about Lewis and Harris, Charles and O'Sullivan reached South Uist. This was Clanranald country, and here they would be safe – for the moment. By now, though, Cumberland knew that his cousin was in the Outer Hebrides. He increased the number of naval vessels patrolling the coast, and ordered the army to 'sweep' their way north

Fort George was built beside the Moray Firth, just seven miles north of Culloden, as part of the military measures designed to prevent a Jacobite rising ever happening again. The fort covered over 42 acres (17 ha), took over 20 years to build, and cost more than Scotland's Gross National Product for 1750. It was never put to the test.

Flora MacDonald and Prince Charles spent just days together, but their brief encounter begat a romantic legend. By the time Charles sat for his last portrait (below), he had given up all hope of reclaiming the throne.

from Barra until they had taken him. Charles's three-week sojourn at Corrodale was over. On the night of 21 June, under the light of a full moon, he made his way north to Ormaclett and into the welcoming embrace of MacDonald of Armadale's step-daughter, Flora.

For the next 11 days, Charles found himself in the safe hands of the slightly-built 24-year-old. As soon as forged papers and a disguise were procured, Flora and her Irish 'maid', 'Betty Bourk', were rowed 'over the sea to Skye'. There they parted. Kissing her hand, Charles said by way of thanks: 'For all that has happened I hope, madam, we shall meet in St James's Palace yet.' It would prove another empty promise. The closest brave Flora MacDonald ever got to the royal palace was when she was locked away in the nearby Tower of London a few weeks later.

On Skye Charles slept between clean linen sheets for the first time in over two months – and then he was off once more into the heather. On 5 July he returned yet again to the mainland. By 9 August he was back in the Great Glen, and on 30 August, he reached the secret lair of Macpherson of Cluny, chief of Clan Macpherson, high on the slopes of Ben Alder, in the heart of the Highlands. Safe as an eagle in its eerie, Charles sat and awaited word of rescue.

He didn't have long to wait. Early in September two more French frigates sailed into the Minch. Looking first into Loch Boisdale, in South Uist, the captains of the *L'Heureux* and the *Le Prince de Conti* were advised to cross to Loch nam Uamh and await the prince's coming. For two nerve-jangling weeks the two vessels lay at anchor, whilst the message was passed along the line to Macpherson's 'cage'. At last, in the early morning of Saturday 20 September, Charles appeared on the shore of Loch nam Uamh and went aboard *L'Heureux*. It proved a happy ship. By noon that day, as his vessel rounded Barra Head, 'the prince in the heather' saw his last glimpse of Scotland. By the end of that month he was safely back in France.

END OF THE LINE

When Charles arrived in Paris he received neither a royal title nor a rousing anthem in his honour, though he was fêted by the French after a fashion. But when, in 1748, the Treaty of Aix-la-Chapelle brought Britain and France to peace once more, Charles was declared *persona non grata*. Refusing to leave France of his own accord, he was arrested and deported. So began his wanderings. Avignon and Ghent were graced by his presence; so too London, which he visited secretly in the Spring of 1750. Whilst there, he became an Anglican, in the belief that this would somehow improve his chance of becoming king of Great Britain. He had still not given up the dream.

By now, though, depression and drink were fast taking their toll on the once bonnie prince. The news that Cumberland had been soundly beaten in battle by the French, at Hastenbeck on 26 July 1757, can only have given him brief consolation, for he would soon have been reminded that the only battle his reviled cousin ever won in his entire military career had been Culloden!

Charles took high-born mistresses, and badly mistreated them too. He also took up again with an 'old flame', Clementina Walkinshaw, who had nursed him when he lay ill at her uncle's house at Bannockburn in January 1746. Although the relationship did not

last because of his accursed drinking, it provided one brief high spot in an otherwise declining spiral – the birth of a daughter, Charlotte, in 1753. She would be his sole surviving heir.

Only after his father's death, on 1 January 1766, did Charles return to the Palazzo Muti, in Rome. Whether it was because of his drinking or the fact that he had renounced his Catholicism we will never know, but the pope refused to acknowledge James VIII & III's son as King Charles III. Charles continued in his decline. He did marry eventually – Princess Louise of Stolberg, 31 years his junior, on 17 April 1772 – but the brandy bottle soon ended that relationship too. As he slumped into old age and alcoholic stupor, just about the only person who cared for him, and comforted him, was Charlotte. Shortly before his death, Charles bestowed on her the title 'Duchess of Albany', the ancient name of Scotland. He died in her

arms on 31 January 1788, a century after his grandfather, James VII & II, had fled his three thrones. The dream Charles harboured, of recovering all three, died with him.

By the time of his death, the brutal realism of Culloden and its bloody aftermath had been replaced by a dewy-eyed romanticism. Even the poet Robert Burns, a Lowlander born 13 years after the slaughter on Drummossie Moor, was affected by it. Shortly after Charles's death, he penned 'The bonnie lass of Albany', in which he prepares to welcome the return to Scotland of Charles's daughter, Charlotte. It was pure fantasy of course, and everyone knew it. The battle of Culloden had effectively put paid to that.

We'll daily pray, we'll nightly pray,
On bended knees most fervently,
The time may come, wi pipe an drum,
We'll welcome hame fair Albany.

The Jacobite flag flies over the battlefield. Culloden was emphatically not a battle between Scotland and England, but the culmination of a civil war. Jacobitism was a flag of convenience for people with differing agendas – for those who wished to see the return of the Stuart dynasty, for those who sought to overthrow Presbyterianism, and for those who despised the Union of Scotland and England for whatever reason.

The battlefield is today in the care of the National Trust for Scotland. The simple
headstones marking the clan graves, and the memorial cairn (see page 1), were erected in 1881
by Duncan Forbes of Culloden, in whose house Prince Charles slept on the eve of battle.

First published in Great Britain in 2010 by
Lomond Books Ltd., Broxburn EH52 5NF Scotland
www.lomondbooks.com

Produced by Colin Baxter Photography Ltd
Copyright © Colin Baxter Photography Ltd 2010

Text © Chris Tabraham 2010

ISBN 978-1-84204-213-7   Printed in China

ACKNOWLEDGEMENTS: I am grateful to Doreen Grove, my long-standing colleague and co-author with me of *Fortress Scotland and the Jacobites* (Batsford / Historic Scotland, 1995), for her helpful comments on the text.

FURTHER READING: The definitive work dealing with the Jacobite Risings is Bruce Lenman's *The Jacobite Risings in Britain 1689 – 1746* (London, 1980). The most recent definitive account of the '45 Rising and the Battle of Culloden itself is John Sadler's *Culloden: The Last Charge of the Highland Clans 1746* (Tempus, 2006). The National Trust for Scotland has recently published a new guidebook *Cùil Lodair / Culloden* (2009), written by Lyndsey Bowditch, to accompany its new visitor centre at the battle site. Stuart Reid's *Like Hungry Wolves* (London, 1994) and *Culloden Moor 1746* (Osprey, 2002) focus more specifically on the armies, tactics and weapons. Finally, John Prebble's *Culloden* (1961; reprinted 2002) remains a powerful read.

The chapter heading quotations are taken from works by Robert Burns, born thirteen years after Culloden. *'Come boat me o'er to Charlie'*, *'Charlie, he's my darling'*, *'The lovely lass o Inverness'* and *'The bonnie lass o Albany'* can be found in *The Complete Illustrated Poems, Songs and Ballads of Robert Burns*, published by Lomond Books (1992).

Front and Back Cover: Battle of Culloden, by Mark Churms   *Page 1:* Memorial cairn, Culloden battlefield.